Trevor Gordon's book feels like a conversation with a trusted confidant. To know the road ahead we have to ask those who are coming back. Trevor has been on the road of entrepreneurship and has graciously come back to hand you a map."

— **EDWIN MCCAIN**
Singer-Songwriter, Musician & Entrepreneur

You can't read Trevor's book without believing success is not only on the horizon, but obtainable. His common sense look at business, life and family is a refreshing change from today's more shallow approach to life and business that seems far too common."

— **MIKE GALLAGHER**
Nationally Syndicated Radio Host
& Fox News Contributor

The lessons and skills discussed throughout Trevor's first book were on full display when I had the great fortune to meet and work with Trevor when my band, the Georgia Satellites, performed at the Rock Out Hunger Concert to benefit Loaves & Fishes. Trevor immediately engendered a nostalgic feeling of having known him our whole lives through his unbridled enthusiasm and down-to-earth approach. I was most impressed with his commitment to share the successes of his company through this philanthropic endeavor, and while unlikely the objective or motivation given his personal commitment to helping others in need, this event no doubt strikes home to many of the business development and management lessons touched upon in these pages."

— **TODD JOHNSTON**
Entrepreneur, Drummer & Manager for the
Georgia Satellites

Trevor is a tremendous visionary leader. His instincts are spot-on for when to act, what to go for, and why you need to be prepared to walk away. His business acumen applies well to both non-profit and for-profit entities."

— **DANA S. MCCONNELL**
Executive Director, Center for Developmental Services

The Power of Pivot. Copyright © 2017 by Trevor Gordon.
All rights reserved. Reproduced in the United States of America. No part of this book may be used or reproduced in any manner whatsoever without written permission except in the case of brief quotations embodied in critical articles and reviews. For information, send inquiries c/o Trevor Gordon, 800 E. North St., 2nd Floor, Greenville, SC 29601.

First Edition

Gordon, Trevor. The Power of Pivot.
ISBN 9798430800567

THE POWER OF PIVOT

BUILDING
A LIFE OF
UNCOMMON
SUCCESS

TREVOR GORDON

For Dad

TABLE OF CONTENTS

Foreword 1
Living in the Pivot

Chapter 1 9
Earning A Title Versus Knowing Your Identity

Chapter 2 19
Hiring Co-Workers Versus Choosing Champions

Chapter 3 31
Gaining Notoriety Versus Building A Reputation

Chapter 4 41
Worrying About The Competition Versus Living With Integrity

Chapter 5 49
Being Busy Versus Being Productive

Chapter 6 59
Management Versus Leadership

Chapter 7 71
Making Good Decisions Versus Making More Decisions

Chapter 8 83
High Risk Versus High Reward

Chapter 9 97
Who Makes The Jar?

Gratitude 109

About the Author 115

FOREWORD

LIVING IN THE PIVOT

Every person in their lifetime hits a point of pivot; sometimes, several. These points are, by nature, transformative—offering options in the lifetime quest to define who you are and who you want to be. In the end, what happens in these points define us.

When I started this process of writing my story about uncommon success financially, professionally and personally, I didn't plan on *The Power of Pivot* as a title. In fact, I didn't really have a lifelong goal of writing a book like many do. But over the years, as I reached different goals and levels of success in life, I finally decided to do it because I had enough people say, "You know, you should write a book; your journey would probably help a lot of people."

It was as I worked through this process that I realized how many different, unique phases of life I had been through; all the while, however, I thought the takeaways for you as a reader would come from the actual stories of the important, pivotal moments of my life. These were stories of success, stories of failure, stories of lessons learned, wisdom and insights shared by so many along the way that influenced, mentored, coached and impacted my life.

While some of that is true, it wasn't until halfway through the process that I realized the real transformative changes were actually locked away and hidden—not in the stories, but in what I call *"the power of pivot."*

Change is a funny thing. Everyone talks about it like it's a wonderful thing; everyone wants it and searches for it and tries to bring change to areas of their life that need it. However, the truth is, change is incredibly hard. And I'm not talking about *all* change—not changing a hairstyle or the type of clothes you wear to work; I mean, meaningful, lasting change. In your business. In your marriage. In your financial life. In your trajectory toward success.

So, what defines success or failure and to what degree you succeed? What I've discovered in my own life is that uncommon success is actually found in how you handle life's pivot points, not just with your actions, but with your words, your mindset and your attitude, as well.

This was the secret I unearthed during this process: *The Power of Pivot* isn't just in the shift from one job to another or from one business to another; from an unhappy place to a happy one; from a dead-end sales process to a thriving sales funnel; from one deal to the next. The power comes from how you embrace the pivot; how you process what's happening in your mind and internalize it, and how you ultimately determine how you'll handle the pivot and what the change in direction brings.

That is, after all, what a pivot is. Ask a basketball player, and they'll tell you that to avoid getting called for traveling and losing the ball, they have to practice a pivot—what they do when they stop dribbling, stop moving, and have no option other than to lean on their pivot foot and decide whether to circle around to the left, to the right, shoot, pass, or even call time out.

Championships have been won and lost in the waning seconds of a game based on what that player, formerly running and carrying the ball around the court but now at a standstill, has done with his pivot foot. After all, he's stopped, stuck and forced to evaluate the competition, the position of his own teammates, the conditions, the time left, and the obstacles against him (all the while keeping in mind what the score is and how far from victory he is), all in a matter of moments. His next move in the pivot will determine in some cases years of hard work and dedication.

What I did throughout my life when I found myself in one of life's pivot points, and how I decided to think, feel and react to the pivot, has ultimately been the key to this uncommon success.

As you read through this book, I'd encourage you to spend a few minutes at the end of each chapter on what I feel are the most critical pivot points of this book for you as a reader. They'll give you a chance to reflect on each chapter and internalize the key points. I hope you'll begin to ask yourself some hard questions as they pertain to your life, and begin to create a road map for yourself. There may be ideas for some changes you may be looking for to get areas of your life beyond where they are now, to attain a level of success and contentment that perhaps you have only dreamed of but haven't been able to realize.

Regardless, I hope you'll resist the temptation to speed read for the sake of "finishing another book" and, instead, pause after each chapter as I introduce some of the people and roles to you with the impact each has had in my life, to examine your own and lessons you can learn—perhaps you have missed, misjudged, or failed to honor them so far—perhaps you can re-frame as pivotal opportunities for personal growth and transformation.

EARNING A TITLE VERSUS KNOWING YOUR IDENTITY

I'm choosing to start this book with a chapter on identity for a very simple reason—I believe that who you are forms the basis for so much of what you do, and that if you don't fully understand who you are, you'll never be able to address what makes you tick; how you make decisions; what types of choices you tend to gravitate toward; your ability to approach risk; and many other aspects of your life. Likewise, as you hit different pivot points throughout your life, these decisions—and the results that come from them—can, in turn, alter your identity.

Your identity is partially established by the roles within your life. Personally, I carry the roles of son, father, husband, CEO, and mentor, along with many others. But my identity doesn't stop there. It's not solely the *types* of people who are in my life; it's the *relationship* with those people, as well. Therefore, identity is comprised of two things: who you surround yourself with, and your response to their presence in your life.

When I was little, every time I'd earn a few bucks, my mom would take me to Toys"R"Us. I remember being so excited that this huge, massive toy store was there, and that I could buy my own toys.

My roles in that story? A son, and a kid who wanted toys.

How that story shaped my identity? That's where I first learned that I don't need somebody else to get me stuff. I can go get my own stuff if I want. And my mom played a huge part in me realizing that. She could have waited until she had expendable cash to buy me something; instead, she let me take that on myself. That set a drive and determination in me that severely limited the risk of any potential I had for entitlement.

This is a critically important concept to understand (and also why this is the first chapter of this book), because as we dive into the many principles that I'll share in this book, I'll be doing it all through the lens of *my* identity. Who I am, who I have been around, and who I have taken cues from or learned lessons from in my own life. All of these were pivotal in shaping who I am, how I see things, and how I react to the situations in front of me.

This is additionally important because you're likely going to have a different lens than I do. Different roles; different identity. And that's okay. Just remember this as you approach what we lay out in the chapters that follow—that your experiences have shaped your identity, and that there is no one-size-fits-all approach to business or life. Ever. No matter who wants to tell you otherwise.

So, since we'll be using my identity as the cornerstone for the book that follows, I feel it only right to introduce you to some of the most major players in my life, and how they have shaped me. Some of these people will resonate with you, perhaps because you've had or currently have someone similar in yours. In other cases, you'll recognize one of them as someone you are missing in your life that you wish you had, and in other cases someone you're glad you don't.

First: my dad. There is no doubt in my mind that he has been the most influential person of my life thus far. My dad was a detective, and as I grew older he was recruited to be a private investigator and polygraph examiner for a large, nationally-represented chain of jewelry stores. When I was young, it was cool to have a cop for a dad—I mean, every kid grows up either wanting to play cops and robbers at some point, and many at some point even think about what it would be like to actually be one when they grow up. My dad travelled a lot for his job, but he was there when it mattered. I don't ever remember my mother complaining or remember my parents arguing about him not being there, because when he was there he was consistently present in our lives and in his marriage.

But more importantly, Dad was the one to call me out when he caught me skipping work (you'll read about that later on), and he was the one that quickly instilled in me a sense of responsibility and the weight of knowing that my word was only worth anything if I backed up what I said with what I did.

Second: Jack. Jack is undoubtedly the most impactful person in my life, in terms of my career. The day he first showed up in my life was the day he told me I was a [expletive] embarrassment. Just like that, in front of a number of other brokers, in front of the New York Stock Exchange. The thing is—he was right, and once I owned that I was able to catapult my career out of simply running around with a big title and nothing to show for it, and into something I could build upon. Today, Jack is still in my life—only now he's my business partner, and he has been since the inception of the Sandlapper Companies. He's still the one to call me out on my bull, to balance me and educate me. He's the one who, alongside me, didn't take paychecks for two years in the middle of the recession, and taught me that building relationships will always trump "selling," no matter the product you are selling. In essence, Jack has been my mentor for a very long time, and I'm honored that he took that moment back so many years ago to rip me down off my high horse and beat some sense into me.

Third: Liz. The first time I worked with Liz, I was her secretary. I was on my career climb through Raymond James and she took me under her wing to teach me the ropes. I quite literally learned the industry from her and in just three years she shaped my career path. One of the most significant things that Liz and I cultivated was the concept of "calling in crazy." Everybody needs a day off just because—because you don't have it in you to push through it that day, or because you just need a breather or some space—but we know to call the day what it is, rather than trying to mask it as sick time or vacation. It's neither; it's just time to regroup and reset. Today, Liz and I still work together (this time, the roles have reversed and she technically works for me), but she's still one of the most influential people in my life and my career.

Fourth: My family. I'm listing them last, but the reality is that everything that I do right now I do for my wife, Sharon, and my two girls, Kennedy and Finley. This is important to understand as you walk through this book, because it is consistently reflected in the decisions I make, the risks I take (or don't), my purchases, my hires, my struggle to balance and master time management— everything I do, my underlying focus is on them. I consistently evaluate my choices through a lens that centers on them. Do they have what they need right now? If I'm gone tomorrow, what will their worlds look like? Do my girls have the knowledge base they need to grow up and be productive and influential members of society?

As an example, we recently purchased a lake house. Because I grew up in Florida, one of my favorite places to be was on the water and under the sun, and so this was a big purchase that really fed into the heart of who I am and who my family is. Upon this purchase, a friend said, "you can't hide money," which pigeonholes the purchase of the lake house as a luxury, and little more. And while it is a luxury, the truth is it's more than that. It's also a hard asset that I can tap into if I ever need to—if the market turns sour or if I ever make a bad decision. It's a resource, and if anything happens to me, there is an asset there for my family that will have sustainable monetary value, not to mention the lifetime of memories we will create there as a family.

In terms of compatibility, I'm fortunate in that Sharon has the same work ethic I do. She has focused on her own career and built it from the ground up, and yet she still understands the sacrifices that sometimes have to be made when you own a company. When you're an entrepreneur, and you have family and all these things going on, it's important to have someone beside you that not only understands that, but is supportive and encouraging, as well. You need someone who is "all in" with you.

So there it is, some of my roles and the people who influence them, and a brief look into the identity of the person behind this book. As you continue to read through, these influencers and champions will appear alongside others, but you'll begin to understand more about why they are so important to the principles we'll discuss along the way. In the end, the people you know aren't just people to you; the roles you play in life aren't just titles. Both combine to form your identity—who you are—and that, in turn, shapes every aspect of your life.

Be careful that the people who surround you and those roles you have are the ones you want your life to be built upon, because they are the foundation of who you will become.

PIVOT POINTS

- Don't ever fall into the trap of acting out a template of who you should be based on what others have told you—be yourself and own your roles, decisions and partnerships.

- Titles don't equal identity. Titles are words that a company uses to identify what you do for a customer. Titles are roles; who you are is your identity.

- Roles change; people in your life change. Your identity may grow, but it will never truly change.

HIRING CO-WORKERS VERSUS CHOOSING CHAMPIONS

There is nothing more important in your career and in your life than surrounding yourself with champions.

Now, I don't mean "champions" in the sense that they win all the time; rather, I mean it in the sense of those who are willing to fight—to do whatever necessary—to protect you, as a friend, as a boss, as a mentor or as an employee.

Early in my career at Raymond James, I had worked my way up the corporate ladder quite a bit, but I was still missing some key knowledge that came alongside the job. The truth is that, at that point in my life, I still didn't even know the difference between stocks and bonds, which in that line of work should be basic (read: essential) information. But then I met Liz.

I started working for Liz in 1994, three years after I started at Raymond James. She gave me my first job outside of the mailroom, as her secretary. It was in that job that she took me under her wing and taught me some of the foundational information I needed to grow even more in my career. After just a few years alongside her, I was at the point where I could soon become vice-president of sales for a national mutual fund company.

A number of years later, both of us had moved on from Raymond James, but were looking at an opportunity to work together again. I remember saying, "This is going to be fun, working together again." And I'll never forget her response. She said, "Yeah, it's been amazing to watch what you have done. It's a great reflection on me." She wasn't trying to be egotistical about it. She was simply acknowledging that fact to herself and maybe to me. She helped get me where I was because she taught me certain things. Liz was my champion.

Today, Liz works for me. It's the third time she and I have worked together, and the irony is that she's the one who taught me so much of what got me here today. It's come full circle.

Before you can identify who the potential champions are in your own life, it's critical to understand what it looks like when someone is a champion, versus just an employee or role player. The differentiator is this: If they're a champion, you can give them both responsibility AND authority. Why is this critical? Because giving a champion both responsibility and authority gives YOU four critical things:

Freedom to stay above it

In his book, *The E Myth*, Michael Gerber introduced the idea of working *on* your business versus *in* your business. One of the great examples he gave in his first iteration of the *E-myth* was the notion that if an attorney and a poodle groomer both wanted to open their own businesses, the poodle groomer might be better off opening a law firm and the attorney opening a poodle grooming shop. Now, that is not likely to ever happen, but he used the example to illustrate the notion that both, when detached from the ability to do the work, would be forced to work on the business versus in the business. They'd have to hire champions in different lanes to lead critical functions of the business since they'd be incapable of doing the work as well as the people they gave the responsibility and authority to actually groom dogs and practice law, respectively.

The problem most of us have as entrepreneurs, however, is that we started businesses in industries in which we had some level of experience doing the work, so it's hard to let go and let someone else champion it with a different approach, different leadership style, or even a different outcome. But if you can pull it off, the reward is this: A champion allows you to stay above the day-to-day issues and focus on growing your company.

Freedom from burnout

This isn't to say that when you surround yourself with champions, you won't burn out. But I'd submit to you that the chances of burnout for an entrepreneur increase significantly with every layer of responsibility and authority he or she keeps. As human beings, there's only so much burden of responsibility we can carry and only for so long, before our bodies and capacity for relationship with other people—clients, customers, employees, vendors, partners, family, friends—begin to erode.

In every case where I identified a champion and trusted them with responsibility and authority over an area of my life that I valued, I experienced a freeing up of both energy and mindshare, and I could then see results in an area of life that I needed to move forward in without the burden of having to be the one everyone came to every step of the path between opportunity and implementation of solution.

Champions expand your capacity to grow, instead of just survive.

Freedom from conflict overload

No, you'll never get rid of conflict if you're growing, challenging the status quo and building a successful organization. However, every big decision that moves your vision forward can only happen if other people are involved. And typically, the larger the initiative, the more people you'll need to pull it off. As we all know, people create conflict, not circumstances. Circumstances create the opportunity for conflicting perspectives, and sometimes even conflicting values and agendas. But ultimately, people determine whether the conflict will result in healthy or unhealthy relationships with each other.

Champions who are given responsibility and authority in an area also free you up from all the necessary conflict resolutions, conversations and concerns along the way. "Got a minute to talk?" In my experience, what follows that question never lasts just a minute, and almost always drains you of your energy. More importantly, as a leader, all those conflicts create, in your mind, layers of anxiety around hundreds of "what if" scenarios that ultimately never come to pass. What if this escalates and she quits? What if we lose the deal? What if our pricing is off? What if, what if, what if...

There's only so much conflict you're wired to handle, and champions free you up to deal with the conflicts you should be focused on handling on the top layer of the pyramid, not at every level of your organization.

Freedom to dream and look forward

When you have champions in your organization, they allow you to give up to go up. What I mean by that is that the CEO's job is to stay in the pilot seat as much as possible and steer the plane towards the various destinations he sees. The more champions you have in your life filling roles and responsibilities with authority to make decisions in line with the guidelines you set, the more you get to stay in the seat you set out to stay in when you started your company: Chief Visionary.

Champions allow you to stay above the organization, dream big, and always be a few steps ahead.

You need champions in your life. Really, you need to surround yourself with them as much as possible. So, it's critical to identify who your champions are. It's the reason why I'm not a sole proprietor, because I need somebody to help keep me in check. When you are a superstar player, whatever value you bring, there is somebody who can bring additional value; somebody who compliments what you can do; somebody who can service and support what you do.

My personal management style really has been very much the hybrid of micromanagement and hands-off management. It's almost a bi-polar method of management, if you will, but I think that's the case for many entrepreneurs. When you are starting something, you're going to be more ingrained into what you are doing. You are the idea person, the concept manager, and the business developer. But as you build and develop your organization, you have got to let some of those things go. You have to delegate and pass them off. So it's crucial that when I hand something off to someone, I know that they not only can do the job, but that they *will*, and that they'll champion that job the same way I would.

But it's not just within your business that champions matter. It's important at home, too, to make sure that your partner or spouse or family is fighting for the same things you are. The trickiest part about that is that you have to care about what they are doing as well. You can't devalue the other side.

There is a reason that every time we have our annual Sandlapper conference, when it's time to take the group photo, senior management is there with their spouses and family. It's not because I want some kind of Kumbaya moment at Sandlapper; it's because I need every person in that family to understand that what we're doing is important. Not like life-saving important, but important from the standpoint of this is how mommy or daddy makes a living to put clothes on your back; to feed you; to put a roof over your head. I had that growing up with my parents. We understood what dad was doing was important and that it was unconventional hours, and because of that he wasn't always going to be at the game or the concert or whatever it might be.

On the flip side, the challenge is this: you've got to be careful. It's inevitable—you are going to have friends that are draining and exhausting. To them, everything is negative; they are usually takers. And then there's the overachiever, who is always going to try and one-up you. I can't stress this enough: you've got to make sure you surround yourself with people who don't exhaust you physically and emotionally to be with them, because it *will* work its way into your business. On a societal level we have it in reality TV—creating drama where none exists.

I get that you're not going to be best friends with everyone you hire, and if you work for a big multinational conglomerate with thousands of employees, there are going to be assholes around, because they were probably hired by other assholes, right? But when you are in a small company, it's important that everybody gets along, because if you can't like each other...if you can't laugh...if you can't giggle a little bit, then people are going to try and undercut you and they are going to steal from you—whether it's intellectual property or money. They are going to damage your reputation in some way because they aren't going to represent your reputation or brand well. But, if you can surround yourself with people that essentially buy into what you are doing, and buy in to your concept—not talking "drinking-the-Kool-Aid" buy in, but that you feel like you are a good leader and a good mentor and a good partner—they essentially operate as if they are an owner of the organization. Too, if you're not the kind of owner or manager that's lording your authority over them, then you are sure to surround yourself with great people.

The people you place around you can make or break you. Make sure you know which before you give them room to root.

PIVOT POINTS

- Know the difference between Champions and Acquaintances or Co-Workers. Just because someone has qualities that make them valuable to your life in one way doesn't mean they are a champion. Be selective about who you give this title to.

- Champions are going to be people who you are willing to give two things to: Responsibility and Authority. If you can't give someone both of these, consider what that means—they probably aren't Champions.

- A hiring tip: You're going to spend a lot of time with these people, so don't hire assholes.

GAINING NOTORIETY VERSUS BUILDING A REPUTATION

When you're 16, you take a job to earn gas money, not because it's going to be a big career-building experience. So when you're 16 and the movie theater has a job opening, you take it for the gas money and the free popcorn, not the life lessons it has the potential to offer you. Nowhere in my limited, teenage thinking was the possibility I'd learn one of my earliest lessons about commitment and reputation in that exact situation.

In addition to working at the movie theater a few hours a day, I had been doing some charity work at that same time—a Toys for Tots kind of thing—and had been up really late working on that project one evening before a shift. At the last minute, I was tired, perhaps even a little lazy, and just didn't feel like going in, so I called in "sick" to work.

The manager called the house looking for me, wanting to check in on me and make sure I was feeling okay. Of course, as fate would have it, my career investigator, lie-detector-operating father was the one to answer the phone. His only response: "Trevor's at work."

And that's all it took. I was caught. And, of course, not just by my dad, but by my manager, too, because her reply was, as I would discover later, the beginning of the end of my tenure in the "movie" business, and the beginning of a pivotal life lesson: "No, this is work. Tell Trevor when you see him he can stop by to return his uniform."

Meanwhile, I had been at my friend's house taking a nap, but I made sure I was wearing my uniform to keep the story up, and I had no clue whatsoever that any of this had happened. When I got home, the first thing my dad asked was, "How was your day at work?" As you can imagine, I started off spinning a pretty elaborate story. "Oh, it was great. A couple of new movies came out today." Clever, I know; I'm living in a house with a man who runs a lie detector for a living. Two things are pretty obvious at this point: First, lying is frowned upon; Second, I'm clearly a terrible liar (and still claim that same title to this day).

Painfully, as I finished winding down my improvised story of how my fictional day went, my dad simply paused, and responded, "Okay. By the way, your manager called. You're fired....you ready to change your bullshit story now?"

I had never felt such an incredible amount of shame and fear in my life, not just because of the realization that I was going to get punished, but because I had let my dad down. I'd just lied to his face and I got busted and I had no out. He knew it. I knew it. It was a defining, pivotal moment for me. So, I came completely clean.

"We were working on that toy drive and I was just exhausted. I just really didn't feel like going in." That's when he dropped a pivotal life-lesson into my lap, and at some level in retrospect, I believe he knew he was training up his son to one day be a man, a responsible, accountable, hard-working man. He recognized the moment, and didn't let it slip away, and didn't pull punches. Because, that's what loving dads do.

"I get that. Sometimes you just don't feel like going in. But you know what? You made a commitment. Your employer built that schedule and they put you on it and you had a commitment. Things happen; you get sick. But you weren't sick, you were just tired and you put them in a bad position where they had to back fill what you were doing. And then you also put them in a bad position where now she has to fire you and hire somebody else. You are taking them away from their mission of bringing people in the door, selling them popcorn and putting them in seats to watch movies...all because you were tired."

I had never thought before about the ripple effect and true cost of my irresponsibility, or about how my actions as an employee affected the business as a whole, but here it was, in clear view right in front of me.

It wasn't just because I got busted by a seasoned private investigator. It was because of who my father was as a person; his character. Here was a guy who got up every Monday morning and got in his car, and drove all over the state of Florida to recover lost items for a jewelry company. He worked his butt off and came home on Friday and then had to be dad and go to band practices and football games and all these other things, because he made a commitment to be a father and a commitment to put food on the table. He was tired, too. And, I remember thinking, how do I tell a guy who's running himself 60 or more hours a week, driving hundreds of miles a day in a car to put food on the table, so I can have clothes on my back... how do I tell that guy I'm too tired to do the job I only had to do for three hours a day?

That day, I lost a job, but I learned a big lesson in commitment. I also learned something else: In the end, it's not just about being committed to the choices you've made, although that's a big part of it. The biggest thing about commitment is that it feeds right into something else that you have to be constantly aware of: your reputation.

Reputation has been a hot topic in a lot of business books for decades, and rightfully so. Warren Buffett said, "It takes 20 years to build a reputation and five minutes to ruin it. If you think about that, you'll do things differently." Reputation is a big deal, because it is what makes people either think twice, or jump at the opportunity to work with you.

In retrospect, if I had thought at the age of 16 about what that action would actually say about me—about my commitment to my job, or my word—if I had realized that my actions speak so loud that people can't hear what I say, I would have sucked it up and gone to work. Fortunately, today, I have a better handle on it since that pivotal point in my life, and I've made it a centerpiece of my career.

In fact, I have this on a sign that hangs on the wall right next to my desk:

> *Reputation is the only thing you can't buy, so protect it.*

What about the things that happen that are out of your control? There are certainly things that can happen that aren't forecasted, and they can really hurt your business. For me, over-regulation, an investor losing dollars, having to deal with frivolous lawsuits, somebody getting killed at a piece of property that I own or manage...these are things that I can't control. But you better believe that how

I react to those things, as well as how I handle the things I *can* control look a lot different than they might have back in the movie theatre days, since the lesson of that day and the associated pain, shame, guilt and awakening are still fresh in my memory.

So right now, I am managing expectations and maintaining commitments and keeping my reputation intact, so that if something like that ever does happen, I can balance it against what people know about me outside of that issue. There will always be things that you will never be able to control, so when you have that ability to control something, make sure you do it right and you do it well.

It all comes back to trust. There is no doubt in my mind that eventually I will end up on the wrong side of a deal, but I don't want to have to apologize for my decisions along the way, or feel those same feelings of shame, guilt and irresponsibility ever again, knowing how my actions have a ripple effect.

Today in my business, if there is a problem with an investment, I want to be able to show somebody that the problem is generated by the market, not by careless or callous behavior.

We had a deal once that we were doing in the oil market, but it wasn't producing the way we thought because when we bought it, oil was trading at $103 and then months later it was at $31. So the conversation wasn't about a bad decision I may have made…it was about how we were going to get through a valley. "There are still 900 drilling rigs out there; they are still generating 10 barrels of water per barrel of oil produced; we are still getting revenue—it's not as much as expected, but it's still there and you have a sustainable asset. Markets cycle and we are positioned to see it through and make adjustments where necessary."

That kind of conversation, analysis, concern, planning, and transparent caring goes a long way for sustaining lasting customer relationships. I want to be able to talk about those kinds of things. It's not always a good conversation or an easy conversation, but it develops trust. And trust is the most fundamental block upon which you'll build any relationships that matter in your life..

Do people trust you when you say you will do something? That's commitment.

Do people trust you even when you mess up? That's reputation.

PIVOT POINTS

- Reputation is the only thing you can't buy, so protect it.

- Don't plan on apologizing later. You can't control everything that happens to your business, so when you have something you can control, make sure you are honoring your commitments and keeping your reputation intact. Then, when something bad does happen, your reputation speaks for you.

- Someone out there is basing their next decision on a commitment you have made. Don't be the reason that decision turns into a bad one.

WORRYING ABOUT THE COMPETITION VERSUS LIVING WITH INTEGRITY

One of the biggest, most impactful parts of my entire career was when Jack, who has now been my business partner for years, told me I was an embarrassment in front of the New York Stock Exchange in 1997.

Pause. Scratch that.

Not just an embarrassment. A [expletive deleted] embarrassment.

Of course, like most of the things that Jack does, it was with good reason. See, I was just beginning one of my first sales jobs with a large mutual fund company and I had one of the best territories for mutual fund sales—I covered the state of Florida with access to thousands of financial advisors. But from a sales perspective, I was consistently dead last. So there I was, walking out of the New York Stock Exchange at 25 years old with "Vice President" on my business card and of course, thinking at that point that I was pretty hot stuff. Jack, standing outside, smoking a cigar with my regional manager, looked up at me and said, "You. Florida. You're a [fill-in-the-blank] embarrassment. How is it you have Boca Raton in your territory, and you can't sell mutual funds?"

I was at least sharp enough to realize it was a rhetorical question—how he said it and *where* he said it was intentional, and he wasn't looking for an answer. And worse, I knew he wasn't wrong. There was no logical reason for me to be dead last in sales in an area that could pretty much sell itself.

But here's the thing: Jack didn't leave it at that. Instead, he pulled me aside and asked,

"What are you doing? Tell me what you are doing, because Florida is a big territory."

I told him where I was going, and what funds I was pitching. Jack quickly interrupted me. "What did you do before you got here?" I told him I worked in mutual funds, doing research and marketing, building allocation models.

He interrupted me again: "You taught. You helped your brokers and their clients understand where a product fit. Do that! Go teach. Go see people and understand their business, and understand where maybe they might have holes and deficiencies."

You see, the thing that Jack saw that I, as a hot-shot VP didn't, was that there was a level of integrity and authenticity that I was totally missing delivering to my customers. I was more concerned with how my position looked than what it actually did for people. But to Jack, he understood that it was about finding the gap, listening and then problem solving for people and filling the gap.

From then on, I never "sold" anything. I filled gaps. And the more I did that, the more I realized that sometimes I didn't even have the best product or service to fill a void.

I spent so much time in my early career worrying too much about what the other guy was doing and how I could be competitive against them. Eventually, though, I started to realize that there was a lot of value in being able to determine where I was better than a competitor, or even complimented a competitor, and not just that I was better. And in a crowded marketplace, it's more beneficial to know what my competitor has, and whether I would recommend it, whether I would buy it, and be able to say to my client, "You probably need to talk to Bob. Bob has a product that would look really good for you right now."

What does that do for that customer? That builds trust and reputation, creates a whole new dynamic, and establishes an entirely different level of confidence. Maybe I didn't get the sale that day. But I guarantee he's going to take a good, hard look at the things that I do have in the future, and he's going to trust my advice down the road. Many times, there is a greater value in being the long-term resource vs. the fly-by-night "sales-guy."

There is, hands down, nothing better than understanding what the other guy has, because it shows you have integrity. It shows you have an understanding of the needs and gap-fillers, and that you aren't just pitching product—you're pitching concepts. You're pitching value and relationships, not just selling something. No one likes to be sold!

I've arrived at a point in my life and in my career where I quit being competitive with the other small, independent broker dealers and product sponsors out there. I'm okay missing deals. I don't care what my competition is doing from the standpoint of "they're selling more than me." There's enough business to go around.

Once you stop obsessing about that kind of competition, and stop trying to be all things to all people—once you stop trying to do things that are outside of your scope and wheelhouse—success naturally begins to find you.

Of course, having competitive intel is never a bad thing, and being aware of who your competition is is very important. But chances are, unless you are Alexander Graham Bell, you probably didn't invent anything, so there is somebody out there doing what you are doing. The question is, can you do it better? Can you do it faster? Can you deliver a better product at a better price in a niche? Those are the things you need to be aware of as you build your vision.

Do you have to be aware of your competition? Absolutely. You've got to have competitive research, no doubt about that. But do I spend eight hours out of my day worrying about John Smith Broker/Dealer and who he's recruiting and what products he's signing? No. I just have to be aware that he has a competing product so I need to make sure that I'm providing my representatives with the right value proposition for them to grow their business to be competitive in their marketplace. That's a much different dynamic and a completely different mindset. And you'll find it's actually quite liberating.

Another reason why that paradigm is critical for success? One day, Trevor Gordon Broker/Dealer and John Smith Broker/Dealer might work together; you never know where two people are going to end up again. You never know who you are going to need to work with. You may discover that somebody turns out to be a resource to you five years from now because of what they know. And then, one day, you're sitting around the table having a conversation saying, "Yeah, I know this guy...

what's his name? Oh right, that's the guy who fired me."

You can't burn bridges. Even if you think somebody has really done you wrong, or you really, truly hate the competition, you can't burn those bridges unless you want them gone forever.

PIVOT POINTS

- There's nothing new under the sun, so get comfortable with the fact that someone else is doing what you do, or selling what you are trying to sell. Once you're comfortable with it, get better/faster/cheaper than the other guy so you have a point of difference.

- Consumer trust is made up of far more than how a particular sale or conversation worked out—it's also based on the relationship they are building with you, and how much you can be honest with them. And trust me—if you're blowing smoke, you're gonna get caught.

- Just because someone points out your errors doesn't make them the enemy. They could be a friend with a higher level of insight than you have on the matter.

BEING BUSY VERSUS BEING PRODUCTIVE

There's a huge difference between being busy and productive, and it's a lesson I was fortunate to learn early on. At the age of 12, I was visiting my grandparents, who quite literally lived on the side of a mountain in Pennsylvania. It was summertime, and I was an adolescent, and so the typical dialogue was then as it is now: I was bored. So, my grandfather, without missing a beat, told me to go out and get all the rocks out of the creek.

Do you know how many rocks are in a creek on the side of a mountain? All of them! My grandfather just sat at the house laughing hysterically and I'm crying down at the creek because my grandfather is making me pick up all of these rocks and there is no end in sight. I stayed quite busy that day, but the truth is that I didn't make much impact on the world around me that way....although I did learn a lesson about complaining and sarcasm. Still, it served as a "pivot point" for me—realizing that just because I was working hard, didn't mean I was making any lasting impact at all.

In a career setting, it's a lot trickier to spot those who are working as any different from those who are simply just staying busy. One of the easiest segments to spot it in would be sales, since the goals are so simply defined, so I'll use this group as an example, and to do so, I'll go ahead and rip the bandage off quickly: Most sales people today—in most sales organizations—are getting lazy. Technology makes us lazy; we are making fewer phone calls than we used to; we are trying to email instead, and so people get a thousand pieces of spam. We are willing to let big opportunities sit in cyber purgatory just so we can avoid picking up the phone.

Then, there is nothing worse than the middle manager that comes in 15 minutes late and leaves 30 minutes early every day. Every company has one—the guy who just comes in and goes through the motions. For the few hours that he is there, he tries to push on members of the staff to get their work done faster, but he's not contributing.

I once had a member of my staff that—on paper—had everything we needed. He was somebody I knew for a long time that I truly believed could do the job, but instead he spent all of his time walking around puffing up. At the point he finally had to be let go, we went back and looked and realized that he never actually accomplished a thing.

Now while it's easy to pick on the sales team for this (let's call it *presenteeism*), the reality is that many entrepreneurs are victims of it all the time.

If you doubt me, imagine this scenario: There's an entrepreneur. They've got this great concept, and so they are easy prey to fall into the lazy sales area. The mentality is, "I've got the website; I've sent the emails, but nobody is calling me." Suddenly, they are sitting around twiddling their thumbs and thinking,

"Well, I'm not making any money, so let me try this random task. Or this one." Suddenly, they aren't being proactive from a business development standpoint or from a sales standpoint. They are operating their business and then can't understand why it is failing.

Or, they'll say, "I come in at six every morning; I leave at eight o'clock every night; I work on this at home, and yet nothing is happening." To get through a situation like this requires a high level of self-analysis—what are you doing during your day? Are you operating your business, or are you managing people, or are you building your business? Time itself doesn't make anything happen just by spending it; it's *how* you spend it that makes the difference in your business.

It's important to remember, though, that time isn't a commodity you get to create anymore of—it is finite. There are only 24 usable hours in the day, and the worst part is that you're not even able to use all of those; you have to rest. But because time is a commodity we don't get to create, we have to maximize what we can.

"Maximizing" looks like different things to different people, but at its root it's very simple: are you filling your time with things that will help you (or your company) grow and move forward? Or are you just filling your time?

I'll use my own life as an example of what I mean. Now, I wasn't born with a silver spoon in my mouth. I didn't want for much, but from very early on, if I didn't have something and begged for it, my mother had no problem saying "no." But because of that, I became very entrepreneurial early on in my life.

Sometimes that looked like mowing people's lawns. I would go around the neighborhood with my lawnmower. Prior to that I used to have a wagon and I would throw in a bucket, some dish soap and a hose and go around and offer to wash people's cars for three bucks, using their water to wash their cars. People loved it... until they saw all of the soap residue I would leave.

But every time I'd get a few bucks, mom would take me to Toys "R" Us. I was thrilled, not only by the vision of this massive store with anything and everything I could want or imagine, but by the possibility of somehow being able to have anything I could want or image. I didn't need somebody to buy me stuff; I could make money and get it myself. That motivation stayed with me and completely eliminated the opportunity for me to feel entitled. Instead, I became empowered.

It also set in motion a desire to fill my time learning. I didn't just have jobs—I became part of companies. At 15, I wasn't just a cashier at Burger King—I strived to know every aspect of every menu item, how to clean the back, and how to run the drive through, or open or close the store. Every job provided layers of learning opportunities that I could always use to get to the next level of that career, and when I walked away from Burger King at the age of 18 I knew enough that I could have owned that franchise, all because I understood the operation.

When I left that job and enlisted in the Army, I got an opportunity to work in the Commanding Officer's office. I was only 18, but I had an opportunity to work on the administration of the troop that I was assigned. It's probably the first place that I figured out that there was a certain amount of power with information. From a deployment, to somebody getting in trouble—it was information I was privy to that no one else really knew. There is a responsibility that goes with that knowledge, but that there is also a value in terms of having it.

After the military, I worked in the mail room for Raymond James. For two and a half years I learned all of the pieces of that business. I approached the mail room job the exact same way as I did my job at Burger King—with a desire to know every aspect of that job until I could work myself out of it. I was driving this golf cart between buildings and got really good at delivering mail, so then I started sorting mail. Then I was sorting mail to different departments and different offices, seeing the things they received and what they used to run their business, and I'm helping pack things up, run deliveries, and run the mail machine. The next thing you know I'm driving the purchasing truck; going back from the purchasing and print shop delivering pallets of paper and things like that, again, seeing the inner workings of the operating business.

Through that job—remember, a simple mailroom job— I got to see the different dynamics of the brokerage business, from the operations department to the sales and marketing departments. The question was always: how can I advance myself out of here? After all, a lot of corporations promote from within, so knowing every job up the ladder increases the value you bring to that company.

I think that must have been ingrained in me early on—to understand the operating business, and to find areas where there is value. There is value to an employer if you are able to do other things. You can step in and you can fill in, especially if you are a good hard worker and have a good work ethic. And with that value, oftentimes, there is also reward. Nothing is handed to you, but often enough, if you do something, things are handed to you—and they tend to have a far greater worth than if you received them after looking for a handout.

It's about being willing to learn, and about being more than just present. Are you busy, or are you productive? Are you making a contribution? Or are you sucking wind and taking up space?

Don't get being busy and being productive confused. All the busyness of the world can't replace the value of actual work.

PIVOT POINTS

- Time is finite, and you can't buy or create more of it. So make sure you're filling your time with the things that are important and that will move your business forward, not just keep you working.

- Learning is continuous and constantly available. Between the information that is freely given and the secrets locked inside industry mentors or champions, there is no excuse for not using every opportunity to learn more about something.

- Being busy can be deceptive—even to the person who is stuck in the "busy." To help determine if a task is critical or simply busywork, try matching it to your corporate or personal goals. If you aren't moving something forward somewhere, dump it or delegate it.

MANAGEMENT VERSUS LEADERSHIP

Have you ever realized that 99 percent of problems in the workplace could be summed up in any episode of *Three's Company*?

If you're reading this and you're thinking, "What's *Three's Company?*" that's ok, it just means you just made me feel older. *Three's Company* was a popular sitcom back in the 1970s—a classic, along with some others like *Happy Days*, *Laverne and Shirley*, *the Jeffersons*, and others you may not remember—that my generation grew up on watching on our black and white television sets, before Netflix, when we had three channels and prayed the President wouldn't come on TV and interrupt our shows.

On every episode of *Three's Company*, the storyline changed, but the structure of the story always centered around a gross miscommunication. In fact, as a viewing audience, the writers masterfully wove expectations into each script so that as we tuned in, we had an expectation we'd be laughing hysterically over the same problem expressed in a completely new scenario. Every episode, Chrissy and Janet (roommates with Jack) would stumble into a scenario where they all had to posture and maintain a lie they were living between them and their landlord, Mr. Roper. Mr Roper was led to believe Jack was gay—the only way he'd allow him to live with two women in one of his units. At some point, Jack would have a conflict with a girlfriend, and Jack, Chrissy and Janet somehow would have to cover, stumble, fake things to fix the problem while not letting on that Jack was, in fact, straight.

The success of *Three's Company* was that it tapped into an inherent issue we all knew, especially in the workplace: that the management of people rises and falls on healthy communication. And that in itself was the humor—the disfunction of people making assumptions and moving forward and interacting with each other without stopping and making sure everyone was saying the same thing.

Now, think about it. In any business, what is the biggest driver of conflict? A misunderstanding. And what always happened on *Three's Company*? A misunderstanding. It's the *Three's Company* rules of management.

The reality is that management isn't easy, and true leadership is even harder. Usually, the way you set a company into motion at the very beginning is instrumental in how it will operate long into the future. There are, of course, a number of reasons for this, but right now let's talk about one of the closest-to-the-surface, make-or-break-you issues: your staff.

In the beginning, I hired people based on who could I get for no money, with a "let's see if it works" perspective. That was the wrong approach, because hiring is really, at its most fundamental root, about making an investment in your business. Sometimes people don't have the capacity or the funding to make that investment, and sometimes it's just an unwillingness to, but the reality is that you will always pay for that in the end, as I have on several occasions.

The same is true for working your staff to burnout. To some degree, you need to work your staff to failure because you need to know how much you can get out of them. But notice I said "failure," not "burn out." You don't want to burn them out because you want people to be happy, and because there is nothing that takes up more time and more expense than retraining. You don't want to re-train, you want to train. You want to train new people. You don't want to re-train replacements.

At the same time, you need to know the maximum you can get out of people, and you can't understand that until you make the load heavy. But that means that as the boss and manager, you have to be prepared to jump in and throw a life saver to that person and pull them out of the mire; if you can't do that, then they are going to burn out and you're really going to be out of luck.

The alternative is that maybe you end up bringing somebody younger in and grooming them up, and that's great if you can bring somebody up and mold them in your image. But again, that only takes you so far, because it never allows you to fully remove yourself from the operational components of the business and be focused on business development. It takes a lot longer. You are constantly training and grooming.

You have to make sure that you are willing to make the investment in terms of bringing in the talent that you need. And, you have to be willing to personally invest in a relationship with that person, as well, and communicate. For each person in my company, if I haven't reaped the full value of having a relationship with that person, then I've failed. Because now I must hire someone else to pick up those components and I have to get them up to speed with the core jobs they are doing before we get to a point where they grow.

This, in turn, affects my approach to management—whether I'm a complete micro-manager or whether I'm able to back away and let the employee handle their own job. My personal management style really is very much a hybrid of these, incorporating parcels of both micromanagement and hands-off management. That's why I refer to it as a bi-polar method of management, if you will. The way it differs is based simply on the stage of the project that we are in—when we are starting something, I'm going to be more ingrained into what you are doing, because at the end of the day, I am still the idea person, the concept manager, and the business developer. More often than not I prefer to be hands off. I want to make sure I am surrounded by people that can properly operate and move the business forward.

That, of course, is where culture comes into play, and why I mentioned above that the way you set the company in motion at the very beginning is so important. Culture is everything—how you manage expectations, how you manage conflict, how you communicate, how you correct, and how you set up the day-to-day functions of the company. And because it is so ingrained in every aspect of the company, it is absolutely necessary as a CEO or a manager that you treat it as the big deal that it is. So while the miscommunication and misunderstandings led to great hilarity on *Three's Company*, it is not so funny in business. We often hear the term "putting out fires" when you manage people and businesses, but you *don't* want to be the one starting them.

Proper communication and management of expectations begins before a person is even a member of your team. As an example, one thing I instituted and bring up in every job interview is to let prospective team members know right up front that if I hear the words "That's not my job" come out of their mouth, I will show them the door. Period. I don't care what the job description says—we work together as a team to move the company forward, whether it's on an operational basis or a business development basis. We all work together. Aside from just accomplishing the immediate mission, having a culture of "ownership" in the entirety of the business keeps all of the team members invested in the success of the business. When you are a small business with limited resources, this is absolutely critical in the ultimate success of the business.

Sure, we all have core components of our jobs, but if one area needs a little bit of help today, and you're not monumentally busy, you better be over there helping and supporting that line of business. The hardest part is that as a leader, I have to show this from the top down—which is why I have to jump in on a lot of things and I have to navigate between the two worlds and set that example.

Hopefully, you've hired people that will follow your example, and that comes from hiring people who are like you. Yes, there is a lot to be said for diversity—you want to hear different ideas to grow and expand—but at the core you have to have people that you feel good being around. You have to have people that aren't going to monopolize your time with drama; people who you feel you can trust, because that's who you are ultimately going to offload that "busy work" to. And at the end of the day, I need to know that those key people I am around all day aren't sabotaging me behind my back simply because they believe something on a personal level that is completely and totally different than what the core values of the organization actually are.

(A side note: if you feel like you are always "putting out fires" there's probably a management or infrastructure issue that you need to address that's a bigger issue than whatever that problem is at the moment. If you can't trust the people around you, or if you've got people around you who don't buy your concept, or people who are simply looking for a job, they can do more harm to your business quicker than you can make positive moves in your business.)

This is where you have the problem with the more senior staff, where maybe they have been somewhere that isn't culturally a fit to what you are doing. Or the rock star that everybody wants—the hotshot who comes in and tries to change everything about what you are doing. Unless you are hiring them specifically to modify the culture of the office, then it should be a "hands-off" rule. No one from the outside should ever come into a business looking to change the culture, and if somebody does that, then that's a problem. That's somebody that is too "me"-centric.

There's one last thing when it comes to hiring: accountability. Now, whenever somebody talks about accountability, they always think about and talk about it in the context of, "you did something wrong" or "you did something bad" so "you need to be accountable for it." While that's very true, it's also a very limited view of accountability. The reality is that you need to be accountable for the good things, too. Share the success; share the results. If somebody else brought a deal in, congratulate them. Pay them. Do whatever you have to do, but make sure people understand you don't operate in a vacuum. And that's true throughout life, whether it's work or a softball game—"Hey, that was a great double play. Couldn't have done that without you, because I am only one person. Right?"

Leadership is what you show your people. Management is what you make them do.

PIVOT POINTS

- Culture is what you make it. So if it sucks, be accountable, because you have no one to blame but yourself.

- Remember that accountability goes both ways—if you're going to hold feet to the fire in the rough patches, you better be willing to celebrate their steps during the good ones.

- Defining your corporate culture is something that *you* set in motion, but it's fully realized through your team. Make sure it's the team you want in place to create the culture you want to see.

MAKING GOOD DECISIONS VERSUS MAKING MORE DECISIONS

If you've ever read anything from the marketing pro Seth Godin, you probably know that he talks repeatedly about the the idea of "shipping." In case you aren't familiar, the basis is this: don't wait until something is perfect—it never will be. Get it good *enough* and then ship it. Get it out the door. Make something move, rather than getting stuck in a never-ending cycle of trying to attain something that can't be reached.

In the startup world, entrepreneurs and investors often refer to a minimum viable product (MVP) approach to product development, where the initial iteration of the product is built with just enough features to put into the market to begin validating its existence and generating user feedback. This feedback is expected and planned for, because the initial MVP's purpose is to begin a process of discovering application in the customer's world, not just generate revenue. In some cases, the MVP approach is also an intentional strategy to be first-to-market, to begin the cash flow for future development and expansion.

This concept works great for pushing products or services to completion, but guess what? If you trace that product or service back to its origination point—the idea—you'll find that that same mindset is just as important in the initial decision making process, too. In the end, you have to actually make a decision in order for anything to move forward, just like you have to "ship" something in order for it to move forward.

One of my former bosses was very good at coming up with a great idea and then beating the crap out of it. He'd run that thing backwards and forward until it eventually died on the table. In the end however, it was still better than the inevitable pipedream he would come up with in between and launch without vetting, spending scant resources to its ultimate demise. It was the complete inverse of what it needed to be. When you work in that environment, one of two things is going to inevitably happen. You'll either end up being the person doing all of the work because you just can't sit through another meeting, or you'll be the person always suggesting, "one more thing. Maybe we should consider this, too." Either way, you'll end up overthinking a process to the point that your window closes on the very opportunity you saw and sought to capitalize on in the first place. And, in many cases, a by-product of this same overthinking is a series of delays that cause an erosion of passion, excitement, critical thinking and buy-in from your team and your leadership.

The first guy—that was me. I absolutely did not want to sit through another meeting, so I just did things and drove them forward. When I was starting out in this business, I used that as a driving model to make sure I didn't repeat the mistake of being indecisive. I took charge of my own life and took charge of my own career, and I became decisive. I was finally in a position where I got to make the decisions. All that power I wanted to have was finally mine, but remember, I had to be accountable for those decisions, and they weren't always great. Over time, I've become very good at making decisions, and I've employed tactics throughout my corporate culture to help streamline decision-making all the way down the organizational chart.

Because of the relatively smaller size of each of my business units and companies, we have always been able to be nimble, and so one thing we've been able to incorporate (especially me and Jack) is what I call the "hallway meeting." These can be game-changing and transformative, and go a little like this:

(As we pass in the hallway, I might say)...

> "Hey Jack, I want to do this."
> ...Jack: "That's stupid; don't do it."
> ...Me: "Okay."

Or the opposite will happen:

> ...Me: "Hey Jack, I want to do this."
> ...Jack: "Huh. You're smart every once and awhile. Carry on."

For us, this has proved a brilliant way of doing

things. More than anything else, he and I are able to be sounding boards for one another. It's a quick way to get feedback from my partner without having to go through the formalities of "meeting" or "brainstorming."

While I love brainstorming, I don't like meetings for the sake of having meetings, and there's a big difference between the two. In fact I would contend that in most corporate cultures, as they break through various levels of success and head-count, this theory applies:

> The larger the organization, the more the question "do we need to meet in the first place" gets suppressed.

It happens for various reasons. There is the fear of questioning authority; of threatening the existence of someone's job; or, simply exposing the truth in many cases, which is, "we don't have any progress, so let's meet so we at least feel like there's movement on this."

Likewise, I don't like conference calls for the sake of having conference calls. I like things to be more driven and deliberate. As part of that same line of thinking, I don't have time to sit around and shoot the bull all day. I don't have time to just listen. Time is a commodity that I don't have a lot of, and neither should you. There are only 24 usable hours in a day, and there are times I'm using all 24 of them. My staff knows that if they are bringing me a problem, and they don't have a solution, they can bet their life I'm going to make a decision right then to help fix it. My wife, Sharon, has learned this the hard way. If she ever needs someone to just listen to her problems, she's usually going to call a friend and talk with someone else, because I can't help myself from trying to fix the problem for her. It's just who I am, and I'll hurt myself if I try not to fix something right in front of me.

However, I do also believe that one of the biggest differences between very good leaders and exceptional leaders isn't the ability to make more "right" decisions, it's having boldness and owning the responsibility to make *more* decisions, and make them quicker than the other guy.

Fortunately, my staff gets it. I had a meeting recently with one of my key staff members, Amy, to talk about components of our HR plan which, while I acknowledge play an important role in an organization, just so happen to be one of the items very high on a list of stuff that I couldn't care less about. I don't like anything about it, but I value it, and there's a big difference between ignoring something vital because it's not in your "sweet spot," versus recognizing its value but empowering someone else to bring a solution to you.

So in this case, Amy has been looking at different options for the company, but she knew right off the bat that this was something that would make me want to blow my brains out. So instead of putting me in that situation, where my eyes are rolling back into my head, she turned into a champion of that issue. She waited until she found the best solution and she brought it to me. That's when she sat down and said, "This is what we've got; tell me what you like and what you don't like." It was a 10-minute meeting, but she was championing the cause of the company by protecting my time and my mental energy.

People like this are important to keep around and near you, because the truth of it is that once you come up with an idea, with a thought or a plan, you still have to execute on it. CEOs are so used to having to look at the big picture of everything to keep it running that they tend to be a little light on details, or dotting the "i"s and crossing the "t"s. These are the people who can help me know what I don't know.

They tell me what I need to know, when I need to know it, but don't leave me in the dark.

This, of course, comes back to those critical hiring decisions, and being intentional during your growth to ensure you have these types of people around you. However, these are also the same people that I make sure understand the essential power they have. Their skills and abilities are going to tie me or the organization to some sort of responsibility or some sort of obligation, so it's a huge responsibility on their part. They understand that at the end of the day, the decision is mine, but if I'm giving you the power to help me make that decision, you better take it seriously, because you are going to follow me on the fall if we make one. At the end of the day, results still matter. It's a critical takeaway to learn if you work closely in an organization with the leader: Be careful what you say, because your words carry more weight than others.

Now, several years into growing this company and 25-plus years into my career, I've found that while I'm still incredibly decisive, I'm not nearly as fast. I no longer covet the success, the promotion, the accolade, or the dollars—I already have all that. I'm just trying to advance the collective of the group of companies that I have today, because I recognize that there is more value in that than trying to advance myself. When it's all said and done, I need Sandlapper to be bigger than me because I will die one day, and if I'm going to build something into perpetuity that my children can have, it's important to move the needle constantly—and not just quickly, but aggressively, intelligently and intentionally.

The reality is that while the speed of the decision is important—you can't languish over every detail and worry about the potential outcomes forever—in the end, speedy decisions are not as important as making smart decisions, but I believe that with the right structure, you can achieve both. I could make 20 god-awful decisions tomorrow and feel good about the speed of my decision making, but if each of those decisions craps out, then I would have been far better off making one solid, educated decision instead. And all you need to do for that is understand and manage the risk, first.

We'll get deeper into managing risk in the next chapter, but keep in mind that it's a huge part of being able to make good decisions fast. Note that I didn't say "perfect decisions."

Good decisions. Decisions that can be molded as time progresses, but aren't going to end you up in the poorhouse.

Organizations don't necessarily become great because they make great decisions all the time. They become great because they make more decisions in the first place.

PIVOT POINTS

- One of the biggest differences between very good leaders and exceptional leaders isn't the ability to make more "right" decisions, it's having boldness and owning the responsibility to make more decisions (and make them quicker) than the other guy.

- Quick decisions are important, but decisions made off of solid information are better.

- Learning to make quick and solid decisions is not easy—it is vital that you have champions in place to keep you informed and out of all the other stuff you tend to get into.

HIGH RISK VERSUS HIGH REWARD

Like a plumber with a leaky faucet in his house that goes unrepaired, I too have fallen victim to the "do as I say, not as I do" mentality to life. There is historical evidence to this during the first period of my career in which I was making serious, adult money and I developed the lifestyle to go with it. And, like most people I knew in that stage of life, I failed to put anything of significance away; didn't save any for a rainy day, or for anything else, for that matter. Unlike the continued reminders that it didn't as a child, I was living as if money did, in fact, grow on trees. I was oblivious to things like risk management, worst-case-scenarios, or how market fluctuations would have any sort of impact on me personally. I mean...seriously, I knew the terms—preached them pretty convincingly and impressively to clients—but in the end failed to see how it could ever impact me...my money was made.

And then, it was gone.

As someone who has spent his entire adult life earning a living based on domestic and global investment markets, recognizing a multitude of arenas to make money, you would think that I would be better prepared for any type of market or economic downturn...I wasn't! When the markets fell and the proverbial crap hit the fan, I was in a bad position, to put it mildly; it hit me hard. More directly and accurately, the truth is that I put myself in a bad position—a paradigm of personal responsibility that most people miss. I, Trevor Gordon, either by commission or omission, put myself in that position by choice. After all, we may be born and raised in certain conditions, but we all grow up by choice.

So now, there I was, living on my credit cards, having made the decision to build my own business and in the worst "lean-time" stretches of it, I'm not even taking a salary. During those periods, I had to do the unfathomable. I had to borrow money. From my dad.

I won't tell you how that ended up, but let's just say that my dad was, once again, a beacon of truth and reality. I knew, at that pivotal moment, that I never again wanted to be in that situation.

Over the years, I've come to recognize common, predictable patterns in the life cycle of a business, and experienced entrepreneurs acknowledge that there are certain inevitabilities in business. One of those is that the market will always change. In fact, when you wake up one day and realize you haven't thought about the market changing in some time, watch out. There will be bubbles; there will be highs and lows. How you navigate them is up to you, but much of your existence, success and future potential will come down to how you approach—and manage—the element of risk.

Risk is a fascinating subject I've spent a lot of my professional years studying. When I say it's fascinating, I'm not referring to the risk—I'm talking about what I've experienced in studying people's handling and mishandling of risk. Most people I meet live on what I refer to as Level One of risk assessment. By this, I mean that if something happens that is out of the norm and gives them a little stab of the presence of risk, they'll evaluate it quickly, make a decision and move on. It almost doesn't even register. But if you're in a business like mine, where risk (and the rewards thereof) *are* the business—you have to learn to live way higher than Level One in order to be successful. The stakes get higher, but it's well worth it, because with higher risk often comes the potential for monumental rewards.

So how do you navigate risk/reward and not constantly find yourself living in constant fear of snapping under pressure and crashing to the ground?

The first step I recommend in successfully navigating and achieving a higher level of what we'll call Risk Management is this: get rid of your victim mentality. You aren't a victim. In fact, stop reading for a minute, and say it out loud: "I'm not a victim." No matter what has happened to you, at some point you have to decide you're not a victim of the life you're in; you're a volunteer in it. If you believe you're a victim, you'll continue to stay stagnant and flounder around. Don't let yourself be easily taken advantage of, and learn how to do your own math on issues in front of you.

Don't fall prey to ideologies that aren't yours that you haven't validated; outside perspective can be hugely beneficial when it's in the form of mentorship and advice, but always make sure you aren't holding yourself captive to anyone else's perspective besides yours and your Creator.

What you'll find, almost immediately, is that if you can shift away from a victim mentality it will impact all of your decision making going forward—how you spend money; who you associate with; how you invest; how much risk you are willing to take.

Then, and only then, are you able to mitigate the risk in the constantly changing world around you.

In my job, for example, one of the things we deal with is something called options. In the financial markets, options are contracts where you can speculate. You can look at any options contract and you can calculate three things: a maximum gain, a maximum loss, and a break-even point. A maximum loss is what's going to be whatever you spent into it, or will be forced to spend if you end up on the wrong side of the option. This can be somewhat unlimited; it's really just an indicator of how much you stand to lose if it all hits the toilet in the end. The maximum gain can also be unlimited, but is usually more fixed, with few exceptions. And the break-even point is what happens if it only makes enough to cover what you put in.

I, for one, never liked options because for every option there must be a winner and a loser, and one of my core values is creating win-win scenarios. However, the assessment itself still holds true—not just for options in the investment world, but for any scenario you are looking at. Where is the line drawn where you know you've won? Where is the line where you know you're toast?

When I was in the military, we called these "go/no go" zones. We knew where the boundaries were and then we were free to make decisions and act accordingly within those boundaries. These lines changed, over time. And real life is just like that—I am a thousand times different now than I was 20,

15 or even 10 years ago in my career. It's not exclusively due to my successes; it's equally attributed to my failures.

It was early on, while Jack and I were talking about a potentially career-changing opportunity, that I finally drilled down to this surprisingly simple, stake-in-the-ground question—and it's a question that I've held onto for most of the decisions I've made ever since. Here it is:

> What is the biggest thing that can happen to me if I don't get this right?

For me, I realized that the answer to that question was simple: I'd lose all my stuff. Well, guess what? I can get more stuff.

So, that was it. If the biggest risk was that they can just take away the stuff I accumulated to that point, but I know how to get more stuff, it is a manageable risk for me. The alternative—if I get this wrong I'm going to lose all my stuff, create years and years of continuable liability, take things away from my mother, kill all my investors—then that's a risk I don't want to take. So, in most decisions I make, those "go/no go" lines are drawn already. I don't have to mull over it incessantly and worry and wring my hands. I just determine its rightful place on the risk/reward spectrum, decide, and move on.

In fact, once I make the decision to move on, I commit to making it a regret-free decision due to my counter philosophy to my sage "lose my crap" risk analysis, and that is: I have never lost money on a deal I missed.

In the end, I've drawn commitment lines, and defined the most crucial boundary for my life and my company: where my commitment to X ends. And while it seems like it's a pretty simple thing—this drawing a commitment line—the truth is that many entrepreneurs and CEOs will fail time and time again by not honoring it.

Here's an example: you're in a project that's going well, until it's not. Stuff starts going south, and it's past the point where you feel comfortable, but not dead in the water yet. What do you do? Well, a lot of entrepreneurs will say, "Well, I'm already in this far, so let's push a little further." Or, "I've already invested so much, let's see if I can turn this around."

Or, the opposite: you have a business buying red cars on Tuesdays. A "great opportunity" comes up to buy purple cars on Wednesdays, and you want to take it because the opportunity has presented itself to you and you think you can make money on it.

Both of these scenarios are dangerous ones. In the first, you're giving up your ground in hopes that you can make something better. In the second, you're stepping outside your business model because you hope that it's a great opportunity, for one reason or another. In both, you're hoping that you can *hope* your way into good business decisions, and that's where so many entrepreneurs make critical mistakes—they will take that company to its grave because they aren't honoring the commitment line they made (or worse, didn't make) at the beginning, when they weren't as emotionally involved in holding on to something that was withering on the vine.

Sometimes it's hard to honor those lines, but I promise you, it will save you time and time again if you do. There are times that I've had so many opportunities—great opportunities that are so tempting to get involved in—but they are outside of commitment lines that I put in place.

Still, the temptation is strong, and that's because the chase of opportunity and money and competition is strong. But guess what? As I said above, I never lost money on a deal I missed.

There's one more thing I should mention that plays into that line of thinking: the fear of "missing out." So many entrepreneurs get so bogged down in all the opportunities that when they see one it robs them of their senses, and of their predetermined boundaries. But here's the thing: I'm not afraid to miss a deal anymore.

I've resigned myself to the fact that I'm never going to catch up to Warren Buffet's checkbook, and I'm not worried about what "everybody else" is doing. My motivation now is simply to create a legacy; to creating something for my children; to make sure if I got hit by the bread truck tomorrow that there will be revenue streams that are going to sustain my family and my staff and their families. That is my motivation and it is pure at heart. It doesn't mean I won't look at other things and diversify my business, I simply don't apply the same weight and value as I do in the core business until I can learn more, measure the risks and draw the commitment lines for that business.

In the times I've failed, there's been one common thread: I took my eye off the ball in terms of the things I'm willing to accept. And trust me, there are times that it is really hard to walk away from something, but it's worth it.

Then, there are times you'll look back at the "could have been" scenarios. While I've never lost money on a deal I missed, I've certainly missed opportunities where I've gone back from time to time and said, "Man, I wish I had done this differently." Of course. Everybody has moments like that, don't they?

Earlier on in my career, one of my favorite things was listening to those who were lucky enough to get in early on the IPO for Microsoft and made a bunch of money on it, but who constantly lamented about what they would have if they had kept the stock. They'd say, "Oh, if I had kept this, I would have had such-and-such," and really mourn their decision to sell. But for me, the question was: did you meet your objectives? Sure, they made 15 or 20 or 40 percent on the stock, which is what they wanted to do at the time. Great. Stop looking at it and shut up, because the success, in total, was not a straight shot; it never is. There will be periods of ups and downs. Be proud you met or exceeded the objectives you had going in, and honoring the commitment to get out when you reached them, because in the end, it's not just about evaluating and buying into an opportunity—it's also about knowing how you are going to exit. And if my goal is to do 15 percent on this deal and get rid of it, then when I get to 14 and a half it's not time for me to say, "Wait, maybe I can get to 17 percent." That's how Vegas is designed, and the house, eventually, will win every time in that paradigm.

In the end, risk assessment is really about making regret-free decisions. You sit down and evaluate an opportunity: what's the value, what's it going to cost, what are the risks we take on? But the critical element most people leave out is: how do I get out of it? Where's the end? Where is the result we are looking for, and when we get to it, do we walk away?

Here's a great question to ask as you learn to evaluate risk in your own life: What is the worst possible thing that can happen if I make this decision today? Obviously, you can't know everything all of the time and we all know that warning about "best laid plans", but I believe that decision-making at its core is very simple. Here's an example: You think this idea advances what you are doing forward, but the risk is X. Ask yourself: Is Risk X something manageable? If so, then do it and quit talking about it. If Risk X is something that is going to potentially bankrupt the company or the cost of recovery is too steep, then don't do it, or establish a timeline for your final decision to be made. Then do the due diligence, move on with a decision and get behind it 100 percent. Don't let it linger on forever, because risk associated with "the unknown" will always be there.

Set your commitment lines before you do the deal. You'll never lose money on a deal you miss.

PIVOT POINTS

- Don't be afraid to get out on a limb...more times than not, you'll find it's where the best fruit is.

- Stop the victim mentality. You're not a victim of the life you're in, you're a volunteer in it. If you're not happy with it, it's your own fault, so straighten up and fix it.

- Not every risk has a rewarding outcome, but the biggest rewards typically coincide with the biggest risks. That's part of the game.

WHO MAKES THE JAR?

Throughout this book, we've talked a lot about finding opportunities, increasing your knowledge on a product, and being aware of your competitors, but there's one more paradigm shift that, if you can make it, has the potential to revolutionize how you approach every project, every deal, and every problem. The shift is really one of perspective, and how you can teach yourself to look beyond the basic information to drill down to a secondary tier of questioning and of gleaning information.

For about a minute of my career, I was a retail stockbroker. Truth be told, I wasn't really great at it; but I was pretty persistent and worked my tail off—two of the critical attributes for any career, I suppose. A lot of the accounts I had were inherited, so I didn't have many long-term personal relationships in my book that I would have needed to be really successful at this segment of the business. Still, I wanted to be a good broker, so I would look at everybody's portfolio and I would prepare for those meetings and talk to them about rebalancing and diversification—all the buzz words.

One day I came in to the office, and I flipped through the *Wall Street Journal*, and right there on the front page was this article: "Campbell's Soup to make homestyle soup in jars." So I thought, "That's neat, they haven't done anything in a long time," and then immediately looked at the company fundamentals and started putting together a pile of information that would help me sell it to my investors. Right off the bat, I start making calls like any stock broker would do—I probably made up to 1,000 calls that week.

I was smilin' and dialin' all morning, when I got to a call with one of the inherited clients I had, who I didn't really know that well. I went through the whole pitch as usual, pretty proud of all of my knowledge regarding soup and all of my self-education on the company and every variety of noodle they made. I don't remember most of the call, but I'm sure it sounded something like, "This company is good...blue chips...market cap out...standard deviation blah blah blah." In the background I heard her quietly listening and affirming my pace and points with the occasional "uh huh" affirmative, so I pushed through to the "ask." I wrapped up and asked if I could put her in for 100 shares, or 500 shares...whatever she wants, based on her cash position. At this point I was still thinking, "Campbell's is a great place for your money" and so that's what I'm staying laser-focused on selling. After all, that was my assignment, that was my focus, and that was what seemed most important.

But all that pivoted after the ask, when I stopped and stayed silent for what seemed like an eternity, awaiting her to say "yes, but maybe we should buy 1,000 shares." Instead, what she said—and I remember it as clear as it was yesterday, because it was so impactful to me—

"Okay. Let me ask you a question, sweetie. Who makes the jar?"

I was dead silent, because in that moment, the rush through my brain was so intense I was speechless. The epiphany I was having truly captured the power of a pivotal moment. If this deal was good for Campbell's, then there were others out there who would benefit, too. This was a pivotal and transformative moment. This lady had cultivated in me, with one simple question, the ability to see those second-level opportunities right away. She thought differently, saw things differently, and listened from a very different perspective, and now so would I.

I soon realized that I went into the phone call with a great idea, thinking I was the smartest guy that was going to call her today. But the reality was that I was no different than the smartest guy who called her last week.

Most people saw the soup—the big-name brand. She saw the jar.

That was the day I realized I had to train myself to see beyond the surface opportunity, and become passionate about learning operations and business processes inside-out so that seeing the opportunity in the jar could one day become as second-nature and automatic as it obviously was to her .

To this day, that's always my goal, and that's what I'm listening for. Whenever anybody comes to me with a great business plan, or great investment idea and I listen to the pitch, I try to pull the blinders off and see what's surrounding the deal. If I'm honest, it's one of the things that helped lead me to see the opportunity in the salt water disposal business—we have horizontal drilling now and fracking was what brought me to the market space, but my jar experience taught me to question who was taking the water. While everybody else was just throwing money hand over fist at the drilling activities, my partners and I looked to monetize an expense. In the case of this robust oil industry, there are, for every barrel of oil coming out of the ground, an average 10 barrels of water to dispose of, and the "big money" was largely ignoring it. Ladies and gentlemen, my jar.

Most brokers are just looking at what's on the table. What's on the front page. Who is the listed company about to move the needle, and determine if and how quickly they can jump on board. When this happens, you end up with a really overcrowded market or a really overcrowded deal, but somewhere in the deal, someone's making a pretty good living as the outsourced vendor producing the jar. Sure, there's a lot of money flowing into that deal, but that also means that if it is successful, there will be a lot of money flowing out. On the other hand, the secondary deal (or what I've been calling the second-level, the jar), is far less crowded, because it takes a bit more business acumen, patience and digging to find it.

You'll see this pattern in the manufacturing regions around the U.S., too. Our region, in Upstate South Carolina, is a great example. When an automotive manufacturer like BMW comes to an area like ours, more often than not, their suppliers are going to be moving into the area, too. The products are so interwoven that when one of them succeeds, the other succeeds as well. The only difference is the amount of attention being paid to the larger entity.

Now, I don't want to be too hard on myself for missing the "jar" moment back then, because in reality, it was reflective of my education, exposure and training to that point. With my experiences and background, I knew success was measured in volume. Stay on the top layer, fill the funnel with as many prospects as possible, offer one thing over and over, and the numbers would work and the activity would breed the app-tivity (applications for sales). Stay focused, stay on the top layer, sell the stock. Conversely, her experiences led her to a very different approach to listening, evaluating and action. It's not about being "right" or "wrong." It's simply about learning to see things from a different perspective.

The good news: You can train yourself to do this, and it's actually pretty easy. On any deal or opportunity in front of you, simply ask "If this is successful, who benefits?"

Sure, the company or person on the face of the deal is successful. But who else? No one can run the world on their own, so who else are they working with? Who else wins?

And although these questions may seem simple, they do require a bit of due diligence. If the Campbell's jar move was a bad move (and I'm not saying it was, but when was the last time you bought a Campbell's Soup mason jar at the store?), then me looking for the outliers doesn't make it a good move. Thinking differently and being able to spot the opportunities doesn't automatically make them good opportunities. It just means you have the ability to spot them.

Keep in mind: Success is really just a result of thinking differently. The difference between me putting an investment program together and an entrepreneur starting a business or taking a franchise is nothing. The difference is nothing. We use the same elements and implement the same processes. If I am building or creating this investment, I need to do my competitive research. I need to know where the strengths and weaknesses are. I need to know where the money is coming from, and I need to know what the operations look like and what the infrastructure looks like and how to maintain a way to sustain it. And there is nothing different in that scenario than me deciding to open a restaurant or contractor's office or a real estate office.

Don't operate with blinders on, and don't get comfortable running only in the lane you know the best. Seeing beyond the basics relies on awareness, and you can't have that if you're set on coast.

PIVOT POINTS

- Winners don't typically exist on their own—they are surrounded by other partners, companies and supporters who got them to "winning" status. Ask yourself who else wins when they do.

- Just like you can train yourself to be on time or manage your workload, you can train yourself to see opportunities in a new light—which may also allow you to see the opportunities you wouldn't have otherwise.

- Due diligence is your friend for any new opportunity or project. Don't skip this step—no matter how unimportant you think it may be.

GRATITUDE

Success is not a straight line. There are peaks and valleys on the road to success, good times and bad. But success is a destination, and one that is different for all people. There are so many measures for success; money, fame, cars, women... being famous while spending money on cars to impress women. But beyond the material aspects in life, success can be measured by happiness, growth, raising a family, learning new skills, or being there for someone in a time of need.

And while success is a destination, an achievement, a milestone, it isn't just one destination, achievement or milestones, but a collection. That is the real definition of success. At times it is fleeting. Other times you may feel you will never achieve it again, or for the first time. But even in our failures we can find success if we know how to identify it. If we know how to appreciate the sun even in cloudy times. To measure our success through the achievements and not simply the material.

Although initially I didn't have a true desire to write my own book, after the encouragement of many I have felt the gravitational pull of sharing what I have learned with others, and so recently was drawn to want to take on this project. By usual matrices I am a success. I have started several thriving companies, am surrounded by friends and family who love and care about me, earn a good living, feel good about giving of myself to others and see the world anew everyday through the eyes of my little girls.

But then again, I am not a success because I am not done yet. I have not made it to my destination. I have had successes (and failures) and expect to have many more. What I am hoping you take away from my work, my experiences, my successes and my failures is to know that you, too, will reach your destination, have tremendous success and achieve those things you dream about—but it won't be in a straight line.

My greatest champions are those in my life who have had the greatest impact on me. Those who have stood by me, lifted me up when I needed it or kicked me in the ass when that was called for, too. My successes, achievements and ultimate travel to my destination goes part and parcel with these people. You met some of them here in these pages. You will hear me discuss them if ever we meet, and if you ever get the chance to know them, too, then you will understand why I know true success.

First, this book could not have been written without the power, knowledge and wisdom provided to me by my father. David Gordon was the greatest, most inspirational man I have ever known, and it was my deep honor to call him Dad. We lost him in 2014, but not a day goes by that I do not feel his presence in my life, and you will get to know him, as he lives in the pages of this book.

To my mother, who has always shown me the value of hard work and sacrifice one makes to ensure your children never know how tough times can really be.

To my beautiful wife, Sharon, who allowed me to follow my dreams in building the Sandlapper Companies by carrying me in those lean times after the Great Recession, when a course correction was needed just to make a living, let alone thrive. Sandlapper exists today because she shouldered the burdens of life during this time and gave me the strength and encouragement to move forward.

To my daughters, Kennedy and Finley, who are the reasons I get up every day, and my motivation to keep moving forward no matter what. They are my greatest success.

On the business front, I tip my hat to Jack Bixler. Jack has been the single most influential and important person in my professional development and in my life. He was the first person to pull me aside and tell me I sucked at my job…but who stuck around long enough to teach me how to do it right, and now we enjoy a collaboration and partnerships going on 20 years (give or take). Given the vast difference in our age (Jack is older…much older), the experience he has brought to my life is invaluable. He has been in the financial services business for so long that Johnson was President when he got his license—that's Lyndon, not Andrew (that's for you Jack).

I would also be remiss to not mention Elizabeth Stevens, who is currently the Senior Vice

President of Product Research and Marketing at Sandlapper Securities, LLC, and someone I used to fetch coffee and open mail for. She was the first person to take a chance on a guy with no marketable skills, no college education or even a decent wardrobe, yet put me in a professional setting and began showing me the ropes. This, in what I hope is her last career stop, is the third time we have collaborated in the 25 years we have known each other.

Last, but certainly not least, I cannot move any of this forward without thanking my wonderful staff and partners at the Sandlapper Companies. We have spent many years putting together a team that operates like a well-oiled machine. The team I have today is by far the best team of professionals I have ever had the great fortune to work with, and one of my most treasured successes.

Special Thanks
This book would not have been possible without the support, encouragement, laughter and sometimes tears with Geoff Wasserman and Jordana Megonigal. I can tell you that, by far, some of my best days in 2016 were our content and writing sessions; but man, if those tapes ever get out…

ABOUT THE AUTHOR

Trevor Gordon began his career over 25 years ago at the bottom of his industry as a mail distribution clerk with a regional financial services firm. His experience since then has included research, marketing, retail production, sales and communications, and his product experience and knowledge include mutual funds, stocks, bonds, insurance, derivatives, real estate and a broad spectrum of alternative investments. Today, Gordon runs several successful investment-based firms in Greenville, South Carolina, and primarily focuses on business development; creating investment solutions for high-net worth accredited investors and capital formation. He and his teams have successfully raised over $525 million in equity to date, to acquire in excess of $1.2 billion in a multitude of assets and investments nationwide since founding his first business, Sandlapper Securities, LLC in 2005. His goal is to craft and develop products, processes and services that create optimum value for clients.

An entrepreneur at heart, he has always had an eye for the "overlooked" opportunity. When the real estate industry began searching for new ways to obtain capital, he was at the forefront of an emerging industry turning real property into securities investments to reach a wider audience. When his competitors were seeking ways to raise even more revenues, he instituted a policy of transparency that changed the way revenues were reported across the board. When the market began to falter in the late-2000s, he developed a highly successful product to exploit on this uncertainty. As the oil markets began to swing wildly, he established a product to capitalize not on the oil itself, but on the processes in service of the drilling and production of oil.

This intentional way of thinking about investments has helped thousands of investors. As the Founder, Managing Member, and CEO of the Sandlapper family of Investment Companies, he does just that. Currently managing eight separate businesses tied to the financial services arena where investors are offered opportunities at both the retail and institutional level, providing investment opportunities for those who are both risk averse and those seeking long-term results.

Gordon is active within his professional industry as well as his community. He is past chair of the marketing committee for the Alternative & Direct Investment Securities Association and a member of the Society for Financial Professionals, and also gives of his time locally, serving as board member and past Chairman of the Board for the Center for Developmental Services in Greenville, S.C.

www.ingramcontent.com/pod-product-compliance
Lightning Source LLC
Chambersburg PA
CBHW052324220526
45472CB00001B/258